Praying Against the Storm

by

Michael David Riggs

Copyright Page

© 2019 by Michael David Riggs. All rights reserved. International copyright secured. All rights reserved.

No part of this book may be reproduced in any way without written consent.

Published by Access Media, LLC Huntsville, Alabama

ISBN for eBook ISBN-13: 978-0-9859593-4-0

ISBN for Paperback: ISBN-13: 978-0-9859593-5-7

To order copies of this book contact Access Media, LLC at:

PO Box 11577 Huntsville, AL 35814, or by email at michael@accessmedia.co.

References

All references are either Bible references or attributed to the author if the author is known.

All Bible references are in the King James Version (KJV) which is public domain, or they are paraphrases from the KJV.

Weather maps are provided by Weather Underground, Nasa, wikipedia.com and Intellicast.com.

Acknowledgements

Thank you to Mark and Michelle Pyle of WFIX Radio in Florence, Ala. You gave me the opportunity to work in broadcast, which set the stage for my being drawn into praying about weather situations, and so made this book a reality.

Thank you Sharon Denise Redding for your work on the cover art. The cover for this book was extremely hard to bring to life and you did a great job doing that.

Thank you Jim and Anne Bevis for your contribution, both in proofing and editing the book. Thank you also for the story you contributed. And thank you for your amazing friendship over the decades to Denie and me.

Thank you to Chickasaw Tribal Elder Robert Perry. Thank you for your contribution to this book — the chapter you contributed and your time in consulting with me.

Thank you Richard Parker for the chapter you contributed, and for your friendship over the years. Thank you for all the great moments on the radio we had together — all those laughs and memories.

Thanks to my Dad and Mom who taught me to love the Word of God, and the importance of prayer, both as vital elements of daily life. These laid the foundation for what I've learned and present in this book.

Thank you to my amazing wife, Denie Riggs, who carries such a heavy load. Thank you for allowing me the freedom to work on this project for the years I've given to it. And thank you most of all for you love for me.

Thank you Father, and Jesus, and Holy Spirit for Your amazing truth, love, guidance and teaching. Thank you Jesus for Your sacrifice that gave to us such great authority in the earth. Thank you for unending revelation.

Table of Contents

Introduction	Page 6
1. My Story of Deliverance from Fear	Page 8
2. Storm Story: The Guin Tornado	Page 13
3. Jesus Spoke Peace into the Storm	Page 16
4. Storm Story: Breakfast At Hardees	Page 20
5. Following Jesus' Example	Page 21
6. Storm Story: Protected in the Storm	Page 25
7. Weather Prophecies and Weather Prophets	Page 29
8. Storm Story: Binding What's Riding in the Storm	Page 34
9. Binding, Loosing and Dismantling the Storm	Page 39
10. Storm Story: "When You Speak to 'em They Turn"	Page 43
11. A Storm Story: Interview With a Chickasaw Elder	Page 45
12. A Storm Story: Jim and Anne Bevis' Testimony	Page 48
13. Stormy Winds That Fulfill God's Word	Page 50
14. Storm Story: Hurricane Ivan	Page 61
15. Science Falsely So-called	Page 71
16. The Personification of Storms	Page 88
17. Storm Story: Richard Parker's Testimony	Page 92
Conclusion	Page 96

Introduction

My life is one of facilitating shalom in the lives of people. I want people to live at peace. This first started with the desire deep within me to live at peace. Though I cannot force others into a life of shalom, nor can I bend God's arm into giving them shalom, I can be — I am — what Proverbs 12:20 calls a "counselor of shalom". I remember as a teenager having a discussion with my mom in which I told her that I was not going to live like some people I knew, always worrying and upset about one thing or another. I told her I was going to be happy and live worry free. Though this has certainly not been the case all my life, it is increasingly so since the Lord showed me in 2007 that He wants me to seek to live in shalom and to seek a city of shalom for those around me to live in. This book is written, mainly, for the purpose of bringing people into an understanding of their authority over the fear and destruction that storms can bring. **This book is written to help people live lives of shalom**. (I will give a detailed explanation of what I mean by the word *shalom* in the first chapter.)

It is God's desire for us to live as Jesus did in His time on the earth – He was our pattern and example. He was also our Redeemer to bring us into the very life style of godliness that He lived.

He enforced His authority over storms and He has imparted that same authority to us. He said in John 8:32 that we would know the truth and the truth would make us free. This book is intended to reveal the truth about our authority as it relates to severe weather we face.

In Psalm 115:16 we are told that the heavens are the Lord's, and the earth He has given to the children of men. Our gift from God would include the atmosphere of earth. You and I as believers in Jesus have authority to enforce God's will in the earth. Individually we have that authority, at the very least, in our personal part of the earth, where we physically dwell. Corporately we have a greater authority that depends on our mutual faith and agreement. God's will, according to Psalm 85:8, is that we live lives of shalom. You cannot very easily live in shalom if a tornado is bearing down on you, your family, and all your possessions, unless you know the One who has authority over that storm and accept that He has given you that authority as well. We need to be people of knowledge, understanding and faith who know how to deal with storms as Jesus did. Knowledge empowers us to ac-knowledge our authority. Understanding gives us wisdom to know how and when to use the authority Jesus gave us. Faith ensures that we do not succumb to the lies and fear of our adversary as we would begin to enforce Jesus' authority over storms.

To this the end I present to you the book **Praying Against the Storm**.

Chapter 1

My Story: a Story of Deliverance from Fear

I have quite a few memories of tornados as a child, the first ones being while we lived in Memphis, Tennessee. One Sunday morning as a young boy living in Memphis, I was in church with my family, ready to listen to my father — the pastor — deliver the sermon. Suddenly we heard tornado sirens going off and we all hurried down into the basement of the church, where we hunkered down together waiting for the storm to pass. I remember going to the back door at the end of the long basement hallway and peering out the window. I could see the funnel cloud moving across the sky headed toward us. This is my first memory of seeing a funnel cloud.

In a second situation in Memphis — and this was one I slept through — a tornado was blowing through our neighborhood and Mom was awakened by the storm. She pulled us all into one room and threw a mattress over my brothers and me to protect us as a huge silver maple tree broke and fell on the roof, directly over where we were sleeping. There are other tornado stories, especially from our time in Memphis, that come to mind even as I write this.

Mom did a great job of instilling the fear of tornadoes in me from a young age. This is one motherly instinct she came by honestly, having grown up on the plains of Oklahoma, and living much of her childhood in the infamous stretch of land known as tornado alley.

Later in life though, this fear became an ungodly nuisance, especially when I worked in radio. Every morning on air I would broadcast in three states that were in tornado alley. It was my duty to keep listeners updated as to weather forecasts and warnings. I carried a deep dread in my heart on days when weather was threatening.

One day I made the decision that I was not going to live in that dread any more — I remember the day well. I was at our home on the Tennessee River in the Shoals in NW Alabama and a dark squall line was rolling in. That familiar dark dread of helplessness and fear began to rise in me like the water in the locks of the dam a mile from our house. I determined in an instant that this fear was not of God and that I was through with it. In that instant, I got on my knees and gave it to God. He not only removed the fear from me but replaced it with an anointing and an assignment to pray against storms. This assignment lasted about 6 years and yielded great results.

I remember many mornings laying my hands on the weather monitor at the radio station where I worked and praying for God to disburse the storms, weaken them, reroute them from our path, or lift them so high as they passed over that they were out of reach of us.

I remember pleading the blood of Jesus over the region of our radio station's coverage area, the different cities and frequent tornado paths.

At times this assignment seemed overwhelming. One day, feeling that this task I had been given was too great for me, I asked a coworker and fellow broadcaster, to agree with me in prayer. Eventually, when he moved away to another country, I asked another coworker — part of the sales team and a person of prayer — to take his place and agree with me in prayer for the protection of our region.

The six year season that I carried this prayer assignment — from the late 1990's to the early to mid 2000's — was a time of amazing relief from damaging storms, specifically those causing physical injury or death to people. I won't try to remember the stats but they were amazing to me, based upon previous experience in our same region.

Something else took place in me as result of this prayer assignment. The fear was removed — that dread of living life on an overcast day, especially with thick dark clouds, thunder or lightening moving through our area, no longer existed in me. It is still gone to this day. It was a life-changing season for me.

In fact, as I write this chapter, I find myself on the Atlantic coast of the United States, in the middle of a blessed, pleasant storm that is blowing toward us. It's not frightening. Actually it's enjoyable, as I watch God's wind and rain do what He designed it to do.

The Definition of Shalom

I have mentioned the word *shalom* already, and will do so often in this book. I want to explain what I mean when I use the word.

Shalom is an Old Testament Hebrew word that is generally translated *peace*. However, *peace* is a very shallow translation of the word *shalom*. The definition of the word from Strong's Concordance is as follows:

> "Completeness, soundness, welfare, peace, safety, health, prosperity, contentment, happy, well, whole, at peace, friendship or peace in relationships — especially with God."

From the definitions in Bible concordances and the usage in Scripture, I like to define shalom as "a life that is complete and everything is in order, therefore one is at peace."

Shalom includes safety and the absence of fear from harm, and that means safety in the midst of weather. It involves protection from harm in severe weather.

For one to live in a place of shalom — a physical place or an emotional or mental place of shalom — means that person doesn't live in dread of weather because they know that whatever comes they are protected and the storm will not hurt them.

Before the storm is allowed to hurt them it will be made to cease.

Praying Against the Storm is for people like me. I write it for those who live in fear of storms to be set free from that demonic assignment. I write it for those who, like me, are assigned to or have chosen to pray against stormy weather in your region or that of your family members. I write so that all those who read, and those who are influenced by the readers, can experience the peace — the shalom — that Jesus decreed when He commanded the storm, "Peace. Be still."

Chapter 2

A Storm Story: The Guin Tornado

The following story took place in Alabama in 1974, and is my personal testimony (Michael Riggs):

> It was a Wednesday night. Mom, Dad and my brothers were at church but I had faked sickness and stayed home.
>
> I don't remember if it was tornado sirens or a TV show interrupted with the weather bulletin that got my attention. I just remember the horror that gripped me as tornadoes came into our area in Russellville Alabama.
>
> I also don't remember at what point I heard that my previous hometown of Guin, Alabama had been leveled by a tornado, and that much of the town was no longer intact. Nor do I remember at what point I heard about lots of people being killed, some friends of mine that I had spent quite a bit of time with when I lived in Guin.

What I do remember is attending one of the few (or the only) remaining churches in Guin after the storm, First Free Will Baptist Church. It was there I attended funerals of tornado victims. I saw many caskets lining the front and back of the church as different families waited for the funeral service of their loved one. I had thought the number of people killed in the tornado was eighteen, but a quick search reveals that the number was actually twenty three people. Eighteen is probably the number of caskets that were in the church at one time, now that I reflect on the memory. I knew six or seven of those who died personally, and had spent quite a bit of time with them when I lived in Guin. Two of them were the brothers of one of my best friends that I used to run around with.

The fear of tornadoes that Mom instilled in me kicked into high gear and I was terrified as a 16-year-old kid by myself on this night of April 3, 1974 as tornados unleashed their devastation. At that time in my life I had no assurance of my position as a child of God. I did not know that God heard and answered my prayers, and, because of the legalistic background of my childhood, I was literally afraid that God was out to get me. I was in horror that night.

That night in April 1974 came and passed leaving me with no solution in sight to relieve the fear I carried about storms. That night only added to my fear.

Relief would not come for years yet — around two decades later.

Thank God that Jesus calms the storm. Thank God He speaks peace into our life during the midst of storms. Thank God that Jesus gives us His authority to speak into storms and calm them, redirect them, divide and weaken them, reroute them... and thank God that He gives protection in the storms that we must go through.

Let's learn more about praying against the storm...

Chapter 3

Jesus Spoke Peace into the Storm

From 1978 to 1983 I worked security for the church and college where I attended. I was working a midnight security shift one night during a heavy downpour. I had, just days before that, heard a sermon in which it was mentioned that God would stop the rain at our request. As the rain fell outside, I thought, "I'll give that a try." So, there I sat in the Chevy Blazer our security company owned, in a downpour, not wanting to get wet making my rounds. I began to pray and ask the Lord to stop the rain. I remember praying harder and harder… the more I prayed the more the rain seemed to let up. It never did completely stop, but it drastically slowed to a light rain or drizzle.

Now, maybe this seems like a light-hearted story about weather, and it is. That's exactly why I tell it. Weather is supposed to be a light-hearted subject. Jesus spoke peace to the storm, and I think He was setting an example for us to follow. We are to not live in dread of weather — rather, we are to see it as a gift from God, so that He may bring food from the earth to care for us (Psalm 147:8). Weather events can be, and should be, a time of peaceful resting in God's care and provision for us.

Instead we have weather stations and networks using what are common weather occurrences as opportunities to draw and keep and audience. They use fear-inducing language and visuals, all for the purpose of improving their ratings and financial gain. Of course, not all weather reporters or broadcast stations do this. During my time on the radio, I tried to be an example of those who do not. But many do, and it works to their advantage — meanwhile their viewers are robbed of a peaceful time of rest while God carries out His plan for creation.

Was it that my prayers that I prayed sitting in that Chevy Blazer worked, or did the clouds just exhaust the moisture they had gathered in them? I really don't know in the above situation. I do know however, that I've seen many instances where God allowed the weather to be controlled by prayer. I'll give quite a few of those in this rather brief book. Here is one example, another light-hearted storm story:

> It was in the early 2000's and I had scheduled a cookout and performance event for my guitar students. There were about 25 of us plus family members, so quite a crowd. We were to meet at a pavilion overlooking the Tennessee River at Joe Wheeler State Park. As I was setting up PA equipment, amps, etc… and getting ready for the event, it was overcast and rainy. I was concerned that our event would be ruined if we got into a situation with a blowing rain.

I was remembering a W.C. Handy Fest event in 1997 in which a strong blowing rain totally flooded the pavilion where we were performing. In the middle of the event we had to cancel. I didn't want a repeat of the 1997 event, so I began to walk around the pavilion where I was setting up, lifting my hands toward the sky, and asking God to seal the skies over the park and keep the rain away until our event was over. As I remember, He wouldn't let me just ask, but rather required me to decree that He seal the heavens over us and stop the rain until we were finished. He did that very thing! (I've used this prayer many times since…) We had no rain on this day and no interruption of our music performances or the cookout. In fact, it turned out to be one of the more enjoyable events I remember in our 25 years of teaching music.

God wants storms to represent His peace by His providing peaceful winds and gentle, essential rain. This is nowhere better illustrated than with the story of Jesus in Mark 4:35-41. Jesus was in a ship with His disciples and He was sleeping. I could write a funny line about how the winds woke Jesus and He didn't like getting His nap interrupted and He rebuked the wind and it stopped. But when I read the story I was reminded that that's not how it actually happened. Jesus was asleep in the boat — the storm did not wake Him — His disciples woke Him because they were afraid. That's even funnier, because Jesus was so calm and in such a state of peace that the storm didn't even bother His nap.

Then, He rebuked the wind and it stopped, before rebuking His disciples for their "little faith." The lesson here is that Jesus was just as comfortable sleeping in a windy storm at sea as He was in the calm. However, He woke up and rebuked the storm to spare His followers who were in fear. Then, He got onto His followers because, either they feared the storm, or did not use the authority He'd given them to take care of the storm.

Either way, we see that Jesus doesn't want us to live in fear of the storm, but rather to calm them and bring peace to them according to Holy Spirit's direction. It's as simple as following Jesus' own example. There are times God uses the storm to accomplish His purpose — that will be dealt with in later chapters. However, to the storms in your life today Jesus would say, "peace, be still." That includes the spiritual, emotional, relational storms, along with the literal physical storms passing over you.

Right now, Jesus speaks peace to your storm.

Chapter 4

Another Storm Story: Breakfast At Hardees

Testimony of Michael Riggs

Not too long after I took on the assignment to pray over the region in which our radio station was broadcasting, my wife and I had driven about 30 minutes from our house to Moulton, Alabama. We had stopped to enjoy a relaxing Saturday morning breakfast at the local Hardees restaurant. About the time we got our food tornado sirens sounded, the result of a squall line that had been blowing in that we either didn't notice or just did not want to pay attention to. As we began to eat and heard the siren screaming, I felt that fearful dread approaching — the kind that had previously caused me to kneel and surrender my fear to the Lord. I immediately prayed that God would lift the storm system so high that it could not touch the ground, or us, as it passed over. My wife and I agreed that we would finish our breakfast — we did so and then got in the car to leave. We turned on the radio to listen to the weather and heard them announce, "The storm has lifted high into the atmosphere…". God removed the threat that the storm had caused in direct answer to our prayer. This is one of the first vivid memories I have of God answering my prayers related to storms.

Chapter 5

Following Jesus' Example

Years ago while I was in college preparing to be a pastor, a man preached a sermon on the fact that Jesus was our pattern and example — for everything in life. That sermon, and his book on the same topic, greatly influenced my life. Jesus knew how to speak peace into the storm, and He set that example for us. Sometimes I struggle with following that example in my own life. Sometimes I wonder exactly how I am to pray regarding stormy weather.

As I'm writing this book there are days in which I find myself praying against storms. That fact in itself is not so remarkable or surprising, since it's springtime in Alabama as I writ this, a primetime for weather issues in the South. What makes it so interesting is that God is giving me new insight as I simultaneously write and encounter storms, so that I can follow Jesus' pattern and example.

Yesterday (April 5, 2017) as I was praying about the weather system passing through north Alabama — as I was asking for direction about how to pray — the Lord gave me new insight. He directed me with these thoughts: "I spoke calm to the storm — peace." He said to me. "Peace — shalom — is always what I want."

He reminded me of Psalm 85:8 — one of my favorite verses — and that He is **always** speaking shalom to His people.

> Psalm 85:8 says, *"I will hear what God the LORD will speak: for he will speak shalom unto his people, and to his saints."* Psalm 29:11 says, *"… the Lord will bless His people with shalom."* Jeremiah 29:11 puts it this way… *"I know the thoughts I think toward you says the Lord, thoughts of shalom, and not of evil, to give you an expected end.."* (i.e. to give you what you'd wish and hope for).

He continued speaking to me saying, "…Fear is not a spirit from Me. I don't use that to draw people to me. It is the goodness of God that leads people to repentance" (Romans 2:4). In reflection on what Jesus spoke to my spirit, I'm not saying that fear doesn't result in people coming to God. It does, often. But it is not God that dealt the fear. Rather, He gave light in the midst of the fear, showing the way for the fearful person to turn to Him. God's method of drawing people to Himself is just to be good to them. Wow! I like that.

As I heard Him speak these words to me it was clear that I was to pray for His protection over the territory I cover with prayer, and to disarm the storm through prayer and in the authority I have in Jesus' name. He was leading me to follow His example. In a later chapter I will discuss the reason why I might have any hesitation to try to interfere with a storm.

For now and in this case, I"ll just say that I was being directed **not** to be concerned that I was opposing God or His will in praying against this storm. So I did just that! As presented in other chapters in this book, I bound any spirit of cuphaw (Hebrew for whirlwind), or any devouring spirit, in the system that was passing over us. I asked Him to put up a wall of protection from the north part of my prayer territory in Nashville, to south Alabama. Then, at His direction, I decreed that I 65 would be a wall of fire and angelic outposts that would disarm and dismantle the storms to the west as they passed through my territory.

What could have been a major event of tornados, death and destruction turned out to be just a lot of wind, and some damage of a very minor nature, as best I can tell from weather reports. This took place in the region from Nashville and central Tennessee south to Mobile, Alabama where my brother lives and pastors a church.

Now I know I was not the only one praying in this instance and about this storm. I also know that my prayers were huge a part of the protection that we experienced that day. They always are! So are yours! The prayers I read posted by intercessors I know about yesterdays storm event were prayers straight from my heart, even though I had not spoken with those intercessors. That's because Holy Spirit programs the hearts of His people. That's mighty good news…

Jesus spoke peace and calm to the storm. He spoke shalom! We should follow Jesus' example when weather threatens to disrupt our peaceful environment. God desires to surround us with His shalom — He is planning that for us and declaring into our lives and the lives of those we love and pray for.

Let us follow Jesus' example and speak peace into the storms we encounter.

Chapter 6

A Storm Story: Protected in the Storm

On April 27, 2011 It seemed to be a pretty normal Wednesday in Huntsville, Alabama. My wife went to her position at the private school where we taught music and I was going about my morning at my home office. I don't remember being on guard or aware of major weather threats as the day began. That is, until my wife, Denie, texted me asking me to pray because they had sent the students into the basement of the school because tornados were spotted heading their way. I turned on the TV to monitor the weather while I prayed. After that it was anything but an ordinary day…

I began to pray first for her and the people at the school where she taught. Then I began to pray for the entire area — this was prompted because so many storms were coming into the greater Huntsville area at the same time. I had prayed through a lot of storms, but I had never seen such an onslaught of storms come so fast that I wasn't able to keep up with them in prayer. Before I could finish framing words for a prayer against one tornado, there was another, then another, then another. This sequence continued all day long and into the night.

Since being relieved of the prayer assignment that I carried at the radio station till 2007, this was the first time I had been very serious about covering a region in prayer. The moment brought me back to those days at the radio station when I had a friend agreeing with me in prayer. I wished for that again in this moment, but knew in reality that this was bigger than one, two, or even a handful of people could handle. A record number of storms blew through Alabama in one day — 62 tornadoes throughout the state, 39 of which were centered in the Huntsville area. I remember the overwhelming feeling of trying to pray against all the tornados that our local north Alabama/south Tennessee media was reporting. The storms became so many and so frequent that I had to just concentrate my prayers on areas where I knew people — family, friends, staff, etc... and felt prompted to pray. It was impossible to pray against every storm coming through. I finally resigned myself to the fact that my prayer assignment that day was just for my family, our staff, and the families of our students. I prayed for their safety and well being.

I prayed for my wife and the students who were hunkered down in the basement of Valley Fellowship Christian Academy. I remember praying for her, on the phone with her, as a huge storm was passing over our house and I was in our bathroom in the center of our house, the safest place our house had to offer. I remember the amazing feeling of relief as she contacted me to let me know they were dismissing school and she was coming home.

I watched the weather with Denie that afternoon. We kept up with where the storms were, prayed for our region, and heard the reports of destruction that had started pouring in.

I said to her at one point, after the sun went down and it was too dark to see the storms — much less any funnel cloud in the storms — "… if we didn't have TV to monitor this we'd just sit and wait and trust God to protect us, like folks used to have to do." At that very instant, the power went out and stayed out for a week. So we did just what I had said — we sat, and listened, and trusted God.

At one point that same night, I remember going outside and hearing an airplane hovering over the back part of our house. I kept stepping outside to hear, and try to spot it as it seemed to be flying awfully low to the ground. Then, as I thought about how long it was taking this airplane to pass, I realized that this was not an airplane at all… this was a tornado! I stepped back outside and pointed to the tornado — at least to where the sound was coming from — and with my finger commanded it to go to the north of our house and then pass to the east, so as to miss our house. As I did this, a surge of wind came blowing through the dark night straight toward me, as if to threaten or challenge me, or lash out at me because the storm had to obey… and the storm did obey. I was amazed to hear a weather announcer say later that night that sometimes tornados would have finger-like shoots of wind spin off them and do harm or damage. I told my wife that this sounded exactly like what I had experienced.

The fact that it happened as I was commanding the storm is fascinating to me — it's as if the storm had a life of it's own, and was interacting with me or responding to me.

These storm systems that targeted Alabama that day eventually passed, and the sun rose to show what historic and horrific damage and destruction had been done all over the state. Over 240 deaths in the state of Alabama alone were reported on that day.
We spent the next week with no electricity except what generators furnished. We cooked outside. We showered in cold water. On al lighter side, later that week I laughed with my friend from Haiti where I had visited just the month before, that we were now experiencing their lifestyle. One of the blessings that came out of this experience for me was that I learned you can make a great omelette and campfire coffee on a chiminea.

We were not allowed to stop the storms that day. I thank God we were protected in the storms. I don't know how many lives and families were permanently affected and changed by those storms. I am so sorry for those who lost loved ones in that day. I know my life was changed, in that I was made aware that I had never really been relieved from the assignment of praying against the storm, and sharing with others what I have, and will, learn about that. This I will do as this writing continues and we continue praying against the storm…

Chapter 7

Weather Prophecies and Weather Prophets

Earlier this week (April 9, 2017) I was reading a prayer letter sent out to intercessors who were praying against the latest storm system blowing through our region. I was very encouraged by it.

The intercessor said things like, "praise God for His protection. Be careful what you speak about the system that is passing through. Praise God that the only supercell coming over us will be a supercell of praise…." Her email sounded like something that came from my heart, and so I completely resonated with what she was saying.

Within the last year or two the Lord taught me that we can be weather prophets and make weather prophecies. It's interesting that those professionals who work for the weather service give "weather predictions" — *predictions* being very similar to the word *prophecy*. One day within the last two years (it was around Christmas Eve 2015) I was casually listening to a major national weather service and heard them say that they had named the winter storm that was forming in the western United States, Goliath.

As I started to go about my business, not really worried about that storm, especially since it wasn't near me, I heard the Lord say in my spirit, "Did you not hear what they called that storm?" He then let me know that we have control over the kind of weather we get based upon what we choose to call the storm system that is coming our way. We get to prophesy the type of storm we want. We can accept, or reject, what weather forecasters are saying is coming into our region by whether we agree with them or agree with what God has said He has in store for us. If I had not seen this demonstrated many times over I would not be so confident in what I'm saying right here — but I have.

Weather professionals do a good service in warning us of what they see forming in the atmosphere and what possibilities those weather systems contain. However, they do a huge disservice when they predict gloom and doom and promote fear, all in an attempt to retain viewership, increase their ratings, and as a result sell more advertising (or on a more personal level promote their own name and popularity). It's also very possible that many times broadcast professionals who report on and predict the weather are forecasting out of their own fear, which is not a voice we want to be listening to with an accepting mind. I think we need to be "weather aware". I try to stay weather aware — but the reason I do is so that I can be on top of the weather and pray accordingly — and yes, so I can disarm dangerous storms passing through the region I pray for protection over.

Jesus spoke peace into the storm. He put the storm at peace! And in doing so He put His followers at peace. God is never the one who promotes a spirit of fear. I ask that God give us weather forecasters who carry the His heart and simply advise, and then join in agreement with the people they are broadcasting to to speak the peace of God into a storm. I am not talking about something that I have not directly experienced and participated in. Remember, that for almost 15 years I was a radio broadcaster and have many times prayed on the radio for God's protection over the region I was broadcasting to. Many of the prayer concepts in this book were learned from those experiences. One time I was broadcasting in the middle of bad weather passing through our listening area — tornados to be exact. I was also monitoring the TV weather station to see the radar map updates and heard a television broadcaster say to people in one region that "…you need to start to worry now…" i.e. the storm is coming toward you. It made me angry! I opened the mic and said to the people in that same region, "No… you do not need to worry. God doesn't want you worried or in fear, but to trust in Him." Then I led a prayer on the radio for those people and the entire region.

For years I have believed, proclaimed and taught Proverbs 18:21, that death and life are in the power of our tongue — also, Proverbs 4:23 which says "keep your heart with all diligence for out of it are the issues of life." Another verse that really applies here is Proverbs 10:24. It reads, "… The fear of the wicked it shall come upon them…" Wow! No wonder the enemy wants to plant fear in our hearts — fear spawned by wicked spirits.

Recently I was given a CD to listen to by another intercessor friend of mine. On this CD the speaker was talking about not giving demonic spirits the opportunity to work. He said something that made immediate sense to me, and that resonated with what I already believed, but he said it in a way I'd never heard. He said, "Demons can only do what we allow them to do. We frame up a door for demons to enter by our words…" WOW! How powerful and how true. As my wife and I listened to this together we realized that this is just the opposite of what angels do. Psalm 103:20 says that angels listen for the Word of God to step into action. Demons — fallen angels — listen for the opposite of the Word of God to spring into action and carry out the assignment they've just heard. It's the way they're wired — angels from their creation and demons from their chosen fall. According to Proverbs 10:24 our fear-based words plant seeds which bring forth fruit and cause us to become the progenitor of the thing we fear. We become procreators of fear.

We need to allow God to rework our thinking so that we agree with Him and His desires for us, along with those we care about and cover in prayer. Specifically related to storms we need to allow God to program our thoughts with His, which speak shalom into the storm.

By the way, in the storms mentioned above, here are the reports: Regarding the storm system earlier this week in which the intercessor encouraged us to watch our words and speak peace and blessing, there were strong winds for two days but no tornados in our region.

Regarding winter storm Goliath the report read, "Winter Storm Goliath lived up to its' name…" These are very provoking thoughts. We get what we believe for. As related to weather, we get the kind we speak into existence. What kind of weather prophet am I?

Chapter 8

Another Storm Story: Binding What's Riding in the Storm

One morning after the storms of April 27, 2011, I was sitting on our back porch meditating and praying and I heard the Lord say to me, "...I ride the winds, and satan has watched Me do this for millennia, and tries to copy it..." I have known the teaching for decades, that God rides upon the wind and clouds. These principles are taught in Psalm 18:10 and — my favorite — Psalm 104:3. I've also known for years that satan tries to copy God. As we know, satan has no wisdom of his own and cannot create anything... he can just copy what he sees God do (within his ability allotted him) and pervert it for his dark purposes. However, it never occurred to me that this was true in something as frequent as storms and weather. God rides the wind and clouds so darkness tries to copy that concept for its purposes. Thank God for Holy Spirit Who quickens the Word of God and brings it to life in different circumstances.

This above scenario is so powerful when it comes to praying over storms. I think the best way to convey this storm story is to share with you the journal entry I made of the instance when it occurred in 2011… here it is with some minor edits:

Email sent on 5/31/11

Dear "Shields of Faith",

Since last Wednesday I have had 3 times of interaction with the Lord about the storms that are ravaging much of the US this season and since April 27th. This is a record year for number of tornados, deaths by tornados, and I would imagine property damage and loss by tornados.

As I wrote in the first email I sent concerning praying against storms, I have sensed that we are in a season of having to be concerned with this.

It was interesting to hear what one of the Fox News anchors said the other day regarding all the storms. She said to someone she was interviewing, "... what convened to cause all these strong and deadly storms?" I do believe that something — or things — "convened"...

I want to relate 3 encounters about storms, the first of which came several nights ago. I was laying down to sleep and I said to the Lord, "... I need you to give me more faith and insight into what is in storms. I don't understand them the way I need to to be able to pray against them like I should. These storms are much stronger and more frequent than I've encountered and I need to go to another level..."

As I prayed this I began to fall asleep and was almost asleep when I began to see in my mind a being that looked like a fat human with curly blond hair chewing vigorously and with a big wide mouth, so much so that a good portion of its face was just teeth chewing furiously.

As I was falling into sleep and saw this the Lord said, "... pay attention... this is the answer to what you just prayed for." I asked Him what it was I had seen and His immediate response was that it was the devourer. WOW! I immediately bound and began to pray against a devouring spirit in the storms that were blowing through the Tennessee Valley and the southeast that night (Wednesday), and headed to where two of our children were in Georgia and North Carolina. I felt huge relief that God had shown me a specific spirit within a storm system.

The next morning I had the second encounter... I was sitting on our back porch, reading, meditating and watching some very dark clouds blow slowly by us, over Huntsville and past our house. The cloud system seemed very calm even though it was really dark, and at first I thought this might be the "calm before the storm" I was experiencing, as I had before. But the calm stayed and I heard the Lord say (to my spirit) "... you bound the devouring spirit that was in the storm... that's why it's calm." This system blew on by and remained calm, at least where I was, the remainder of the day. It's like the prayer I pray so often when we have storms coming through: "... Lord, let this storm just be calm soothing winds and soft refreshing rain…"

> *As I thought more on this, I didn't feel that a devouring spirit was the only spirit that could possess a storm, but that it was the one related to this storm and the ones Alabama has experienced this season. It was then that the Lord invaded my thoughts again and said, "...I ride the winds, and satan has watched me do this and tries to copy it..." ([Ps. 18:10](); my favorite is [Ps. 104:3]()). As we know, satan has no wisdom of his own and cannot create anything... he can just copy what he sees God do (within his ability allotted him) and pervert it for his dark purposes. I went in and shared this with Denie... she and I agreed, "...this is powerful..." This is a very powerful strategy as we war against storms that the enemy tries to hijack for his destructive purposes.*
>
> *~Michael Riggs*

I've shared 2 of 3 encounters that are mentioned in the above journal. I'll share the 3rd in a later chapter.

We have an enemy who is very real. He/they are spirit entities just like the God we serve and the Holy Spirit Who guides, teaches and directs us. Unlike God, they are unholy, totally depraved and filled with rebellion, sin, darkness and destruction. They try to mimic God, but they cannot mimic His life-giving power — nor can they mimic the authority and power He has granted to us.

Let us use that power and authority to thwart the kingdom of darkness and enforce the Kingdom of God and His light.

A Secondary Storm Story

I shared the above situation with a lady at Glory of Zion — a ministry we're connected with in the Dallas, Texas area — while at a conference there. A year later I saw her again and she shared with me how she tried this strategy and it worked. In other words, she bound the devouring spirit in a storm that was headed her way and the storm was stopped or calmed. She was very excited, as was I... and still am.

Chapter 9

Binding, Loosing and Dismantling the Storm

Most of my life I remember hearing of the Biblical terms *binding and loosing*. I had heard it glibly, as a child, as preachers in church would read passages that contain Jesus' statements about binding and/or loosing the enemy, or bad things. As a young preacher I would read those same passages, or hear others mention them, and basically just read right past them without giving them any thought — just as I did with the Bible's teaching on the gifts of the Spirit, or the ascension gifts, or any teaching that did not fit my frame of reference and understanding.

In 1993 I was going through a season in which God was reconstructing the foundation that my life had been built upon, at least as far as ministry and service to Him is concerned. It was during that time that I began to be very intrigued with the concept Jesus taught, that we have His authority to bind or to loose anything… ANYTHING! As I began to develop an interest in this teaching I also began to hear, or notice, Christian people making light of this concept, or making fun of those you used it.

I also have heard a few people teach that this authority to bind and loose is very misunderstood and abused among people that use it. Those people then proceeded to teach their very limited and restricted view of this doctrine as being "the only right way to do it".

The truth is, Jesus very simply gave us very broad authority to stop — or start, set free, bind or leave alone, loose off of or rid ourselves of, any situation we find ourselves — or others in. In Matthew 16:19 and again in Matthew 18:18 Jesus taught that whatsoever we bind in earth will be bound in heaven and whatsoever we loose on earth will be loosed in heaven. We have the authority or the power, from Jesus Himself, to bind anything and stop it from performing it's task — to bind anything of God to someone or place—to loose anything from off us, our family and loved ones, those we're ministering to, or our region we serve — or to loose or unleash the blessing of God onto someone, some group of people, or a place. The only thing that limits us in our use of this authority is our faith, or lack thereof. It is important here to remember the source of faith — faith is a gift from God. It is associated with His light. As God gives light to a situation and then faith to deal with it, we then have His authority to do so.

As related to storms, we have the power in Jesus' name to stop, redirect, break up storms and command them to obey the will of God. I have heard it said of Jesus' teaching that "…whatsoever we bind (or loose) on earth shall be bound in heaven…" actually means whatever we bind or loose on earth is what is already bound, or loosed, in heaven.

This does not contradict or weaken the teaching or the above mentioned level of authority — it actually confirms it. We have nothing that has not already been given to us by God (1 Corinthians 4:7). God predetermines everything. We are His agents in the earth to call down the things He wants activated in the earth. As Jesus bound the wind in His hands, stopped the storm and brought peace to the seas, we too can do the same in His name and with His authority.

Further, (and this is a reference to the previous chapter) since demonic spirits mimic what they've seen God do in riding the clouds and winds, we have the authority to bind any entity riding on a storm cloud and stop its devastation, IF and when Holy Spirit gives us discernment as to what that entity is. This is what happened with me in the storm story chapter called *Storm Story: Binding What's Riding in the Storm* previously in this book. In the case I write about in that chapter, the entity was a devouring spirit that I have since learned to call by it's Hebrew Biblical name, *akal*. God often has me define demonic entities by their Hebrew name, as it is my belief that this is the language He used to create all things, and the language Adam used when God had him give names to the creatures He had made. There is another entity that I am sure often rides the storms, especially tornados and hurricanes — probably two entities. The Hebrew names of these are *ca'ar and cuwphah*, both with an *s* sound. Both mean *whirlwind*. These entities are vert interesting… I talk more about them in another chapter.

For the sake of this chapter, suffice it to say that we have the authority as believers in Jesus, through His name, to bind these demonic forces working in the wind and clouds and stop, or redirect, their work.

This is the same manner in which God will send the angel to bind satan with a chain and shut down his work of deception for 1000 years (Revelation 20:1-4).

May God, through His Spirit in you, give you the discernment to know what you're facing the next time you face a storm, so you will know what to use Jesus' authority over in the situation. You will be amazed at the working of God through you as you submit to Him as His vessel and continue praying against the storm.

Chapter 10

Another Storm Story: "When You Speak to 'em They Turn"

After the storms of April 27, 2011 in Alabama, there were many conversations had by many people reliving what had happened. Many of my conversations were with the Lord asking what, if anything, could have been done to prevent such a day. I had been in a state of "seeking a city of shalom" for my city of Huntsville and the surrounding area since 2007. These storms really rocked me, as they brought anything but shalom to our region. They probably were very influential in meetings my wife and I started later that year, the focus of which were about seeking for our region to be a place of shalom in which to live, just as Jeremiah 29:7 commands to do.

One of the conversations I had after the 2011 storms was with a friend named Charlie. It was a brief conversation but very powerful. I was talking with him about some of my experiences with the storms, on both April 27th and storms in general. His reply to me was pretty amazing — he said, "When you speak to 'em they'll turn or change directions." I asked him if he had experienced that on that day — April 27, 2011 — and he told me that he had.

Charlie's statement was a great confirmation to me of the truth that I'm writing about in this book. Charlie is a man of not many words, but not many of his are wasted words, and all of them are generally in truth (as opposed to being in jest). He has worked for many years in the space program in Huntsville, Alabama as an engineer and probably has amazing understanding of the atmosphere and things related to weather.

So, as stated by a man of few words but a man of wise words, regarding storms: "When you speak to them they turn or change directions."

Sounds like Jesus to me… Let Him guide you by His Spirit as you continue to pray against the storm.

Chapter 11

A Storm Story: Interview With a Chickasaw Elder

Near the completion of this book I was privileged to become acquainted with Robert Perry, an elder of the Chickasaw Nation — a Native American tribe in the United States.

To say that our conversations have been interesting is such an understatement. In my first meeting with him I heard him speak about the altering of weather, and how he had been a part of seeing storms disbursed and ended. I made up my mind that I had to talk with him before I completed this book.

We met to talk about his perspective of weather on April 26, 2018. I first asked him about the "Native American" perspective on weather, and his reply made me immediately realize how I had mistakenly stereotyped American Indians. He simply said that there was no general Native American perspective on weather because they are so diverse, with over 500 tribes and 6 factions of tribes. He then related his own personal perspective, as an experienced Chickasaw Tribal Elder and Native American historian, with the following:

Elder Perry's wedding had been planned as a sunrise wedding, but on the day of the wedding weather was threatening. People were sure that the outdoor sunrise wedding would be interrupted by rain and severe weather. He talked about how funny it was that people were standing with their umbrellas in the sunshine at sunrise (as the weather had abated in answer to request or command).

He also related the following with a story who's character's name must remain confidential:

> He stated that one famous Chickasaw chief would use his hands to split the clouds. He'd hold his hands together sort of in a prayer posture then point them to the cloud system to split it — divide it so that it would go around him and his people to the right and left but not hurt them.

This last story reminds me of the one in the previous chapter, and is why I put this chapter where I've chosen. Mr. Perry talked a lot with me that day about authority — the authority we were given by the Creator at Creation. The two above storm stories in the 2 above chapters should encourage anyone reading that you have great authority, given by your Creator, over the elements that would do you harm. You are His highest creation! The elements are His creation, but He's given you authority over them. This authority was interrupted at the fall of man in the Garden of Eden, but is still resident in man. It is only interrupted because of our disconnection from the Creator.

In Jesus, faith is planted, ignited and activated so that the life of God is again active in us. Use your authority in Jesus' name over that which would bring harm to you and those in your realm authority.

Jesus said in Luke 10:19, "Behold I give you power… and nothing shall by any means hurt you." Power is the Greek word *exousia* and, in addition to power, means *privilege, capacity, mastery, superhuman, authority, jurisdiction.* **Use your authority, given you by Jesus, to protect what is in your jurisdiction and possession, as you continue to pray against the storm.**

Chapter 12

Another Storm Story: Jim and Anne Bevis' Testimony

The following is a story that I heard Jim and Anne Bevis, friends of ours for years, tell from one of their ministry trips:

Anne writes…

> "The way I remember this story… we were in Mississippi hosting a Conference on repentance and reconciliation involving the Choctaw Native Americans. We were in a meeting place when the Civil Defense called us and said, 'A tornado is headed your way. Get the people to a shelter ASAP.' The atmosphere was charged with lightning… thunder and darkness all around. Clouds seemed to be rolling on the ground. We had no place to flee. Our guest speaker, Kjell Sjoberg from Sweden, a mighty man of God and prayer — stepped up to the podium, raised is fist toward Heaven and prayed in his strong Swedish accent, 'TOR-NADO, If you be from God come and do your work. BUT IF NOT FROM GOD, SPIN YOURSELF OUT.' The Civil Defense later reported, 'as we watched the radar tracking the tornado it literally turned 360 degrees and spun itself out in a pine thicket!!!'

We saw a mighty move of God that weekend. Even the weather responds to His children's prayers and authority in the name of Jesus."

Psalm 148:8 teaches us that stormy winds are commanded to obey the voice of God. The obvious example from Anne's story is, do not pray against the storm that God has established to fulfill His Word — we should never do that. But if the storm is not of God then we have Jesus' authority over it — to stop it, redirect it, or dismantle it.

Chapter 13

Stormy Winds That Fulfill God's Word

Can we ever work against God in praying against a storm?

How awful it would be to pray and stop a storm that God had allowed, and was using as a tool to bring someone to Himself, then that person die and go to hell for all eternity. In other words, there are times to stop a storm. Then there are times to pray for protection during a storm. God chooses to use what He knows will be the most effective thing to accomplish His will. He sometimes uses stormy winds to accomplish His directives (Psalm 148:8).

There is also a time when God, in His sovereignty, may use a storm to take someone home to be with Him. He did this with Elijah. This was very traumatic for Elisha at first, and I'm sure for Elijah's family and circle of friends. But it quickly yielded a double portion increase in the legacy Elijah had left and what He had sown, in the life of Elisha, and in results God achieved for His Kingdom's work and purpose.

A similar thing may have been what God used to take Enoch home. We have to remember that the death of His saints is precious in the eyes of the Lord (Psalm 116:15).

Sometimes He's just ready for one of His own to come home.

However, there's another reason to NOT pray against a storm at times...

God does use Storms To Bring Judgement

Proverbs 1:27 paints a picture of God using a whirlwind to bring about destruction and desolation. If anyone has trouble equating this with a loving God, then they do not understand Him and His love for His Son and His covenant people — nor do they understand His commitment to keep His Word.

With this in mind I want to talk about an encounter I had regarding the storms that blew through Alabama on April 2 2011, one of three such encounters. The following is an email I sent out to a group of regional intercessors in Huntsville, Alabama sometime between 2011 and 2012 regarding that encounter:

> Yesterday we were preparing to drive to visit the US office of International Christian Embassy Jerusalem. We support their ministry and I felt drawn to just step onto their property and pray. With this in mind I felt the Lord lead me to reread Psalm 83, the passage about those who want to annihilate Israel and wipe the memory of their name from the earth...

… it's one of those Bible passages that reads like a current issue of a newspaper's "world" section today.

When I came to verse 15 I was intrigued. This verse says, regarding those who would destroy Israel or have an anti covenant bent or mentality, *"...So persecute them with thy tempest, and make them afraid with thy storm."* I began to look further at additional translations and was blown away (not the best choice of words... no pun intended) when I saw R.K. Harrison's version ("The Psalms for Today: A New Translation from the Hebrew into Current English") that reads, "... terrify them by your tornado." At first I thought this was probably a very coincidental paraphrase, but after doing my own word study on the Hebrew word for storm I found that it is completely accurate — the word is translated "whirlwind". It is the word "cuwphaw" and begins with the Hebrew letter samekh, which has a pictorial design of a swirling or circular motion. The pictorial symbol has great bearing in understanding the meaning of Hebrew words, as the letters originated as symbols or pictures drawn to communicate a thought. For complete honesty and truthful interpretation I will say that several translations use the word "hurricane" instead of storm (including Young's, Darby, the English Standard Version and the RSV).

What is evident to me though, is the fact that we have Biblical proof that these storms can be tied to that which is opposed to God's covenant plan with Israel. It has been, then, Biblically prophesied that tornados, hurricanes or whirlwinds, will come over those who fight God's covenant plan with Israel, and it is recorded in Psalm 83:15. This at least gives us a starting point in interceding about these storms.

Personally, I believe God is showing that the wave after wave of storms that have blown across the mid south since April 27th (2011) have to do with an anti Israel, anti covenant, root. This is actually rooted in an anti Christ spirit, because Christ was born a Jew and satan has always tried to persecute Abraham's seed to try to kill the Christ. As much as America has done to help re-establish Israel as a nation and help and protect her, the United States, (at the time of this writing) from the top down, is contaminated with anti covenant roots. They use pro-Israel language yet try to build up and establish nations which hate Israel., and seek her destruction. This is a manifestation of anti-covenant mindsets... it represents a surrender and submission to the same demonic powers that want to annihilate the people of Israel. (NOTE: This was originally written during a time when there was an anti Israeli administration in Washington, D.C., again between 2011 and 2012.)

I have wondered why Alabama took such a blow, with all of our early and leading commitment to Israel. I believe it is because of the foundation of freemasonry in our state's history. I AM SURE that the demonic powers hidden in freemasonry are the same ones associated with the Prince of Persia and the strongholds behind those who hate Israel. I have learned this by experience in the process of conducting our business in the region we live and do the work God has called my wife and I to, and through Holy Spirit led intercession. I have no doubt that this assessment is on target. God is taking His plum line of righteousness and aligning the body of Christ in Alabama correctly on His cornerstone foundation of Jesus Christ. All that can be shaken is being shaken, into it's proper place. Freemasonry is about building building — that's its' root and is reflected in its' symbolism — but it is on an anti-Christ foundation — an anti covenant foundation. I had this visualized to me again the other day. Denie (my wife) and I were at Sam's Club and parked behind a vehicle that had a license plate that alluded to the blessing of God, and just above and beside it masonic emblems. There are components of the "good ole boy" network that must be uprooted from the foundation God is building. God is purging His people from things in our roots of hidden darkness. A mixed foundation will not endure (Daniel 2:34)!

God is aligning His building with His plum line of righteousness onto the foundation that Jesus laid (Isaiah 28:15-18).

I've wondered much about how God has blessed the United States as He has when our roots are so steeped in freemasonry, such a demonic religion. (There is so much documentation of this in America's foundation, and proof of it in every place you visit in this nation.) It is akin to the way He used Martin Luther to bring the church out of a dead religion of works and idolatry, but yet when you study Martin Luther you see such strong anti Semitism in him, and such incomplete truth, all of which God has continued to purge and correct in His church.

As to the city of Huntsville and our region, there are two things in my mind that I believe would help bring the body of Christ in this region to a new level of faith and victory over the strongholds of idolatry and death that are enthroned in freemasonry. First, I believe someone with an apostolic authority, either regionally or in the body of Christ as a whole, should decree that we as the body of Christ in this region are renouncing freemasonry and the historic place it has in our state's history, and that we are stepping out from under the bondage and control of that religious structure and acknowledging the freedom we have in Christ Jesus and His shed blood from any influence or hindrance that structure of darkness has had on the body of Christ here locally. I believe this should be done in a corporate way and not just by one person alone. Secondly, it has been my feeling for some time now that we as Christians should petition the mayor, or state or local authorities, to have erected jointly with the historic marker downtown that states that the first Masonic lodge in Alabama was located here, a marker that states that there are many Christian believers in this city who grieve over this fact and have repented for the fact that our early city fathers embraced this system of false worship. I don't know where to begin with that step — but someone does, and I think it is a step that should be taken and that will make statements in the natural realm and have resounding results in the heavens.

I hope these points are helpful to you as you continue to stand in the gap for our city and area, our nation, and the nations. They have given me amazing clarity in prayer and war in the spirit realm...

God bless you,

Michael

The above was an email written to city intercessors in Alabama and Tennessee in 2012 or 2013. It makes some strong negative statements about freemasonry which are not explained or elaborated upon, because the audience I was writing to was by and large aware of the statements I was making and the reasons I was making them. I want to explain some of those statements here for the purposes of this book. I have come to believe that sun worship is what I call "the world's first and great pagan religion." I believe it is a demonic religion… I actually believe it is the worship of Lucifer. I believe sun worship goes to the heart of what Romans chapter one decries when it talks of those who "… worship the creature rather than the Creator" — the Bible says that eventually God gives those people up to a reprobate mind to do as their lusts dictate, and to receive the rewards of their deeds. Freemasonry is, very simply put, sun worship — it at the very least contains many components of sun worship. I do not believe that all freemasons are sun worshipers knowingly, and certainly not worshipers of Lucifer knowingly. I do believe that there are those in the higher levels (degrees) of freemasonry who are, and that they know full well who they are worshipping. I had heard and read that freemasonry was a system of sun worship, but after I accepted an invitation to tour a masonic hall I had no doubt. The symbols of sun worship were prevalent and blatant. Even copies of the Bible had gold emblems of the sun — the "face of the sun" — on the cover of the Bible. This appeared to me to make a statement that, "we (freemasons) will tolerate and/or accept what the Bible says but only as it comes under submission to sun worship".

Sun worship is strong idolatry — it is also the root of violence and sexual perversion and promotes such wherever it exists. God detests sun worship and warns us against it in the Bible. He is so strongly against it that He even included commands against it in the Ten Commandments (Exodus 20:3-5). The system of sun worship is a false system of worship that God will judge. God has begun His eternal end time judgement against sun worship. He has declared war against sun worship, and any society that tolerates it will be a recipient of that judgement.

There are times — most of the time I believe — we are to pray against the storms. Then there are times we are to take shelter under the wings of Jehovah and let Him do what He's sending, or allowing, His winds to do (Psalm 148:8).

Another example of this is taught in Proverbs 10:25. This verse says, *"... as the whirlwind (cuphah) passes, so is the wicked (rasha) no more, but the righteous is an everlasting foundation."* From this verse it is easy to see that it is God's intent that the wicked pass away as the whirlwind. But if you study original Hebrew verbiage, there is no word in this verse for "as the". In Hebrew the verse most accurately reads, "whirlwind passes, wicked no more..." I believe there is a teaching in this verse that God intends to use the whirlwind to do away with "rasha", *rasha* being the Hebrew word for *evil*, but also being rooted in idolatry and covenant breaking (a topic I discuss briefly below).

I'll end this chapter with a reference Jeremiah 30:23 which says, *"Behold, the whirlwind of the Lord goes forth with fury, a continuing whirlwind: it shall fall with pain upon the head of the wicked. The fierce anger of the Lord shall not return, until he has done it, and until he has performed the intents of His heart..."* The Hebrew word for *wicked* in this passage is the word *rasha*. Again, the word *rasha* is the common word in Hebrew translated *wicked*. The most interesting thing about this to me is that the Hebrew word for *evil* is the word *ra*. Ra is also the name of the Egyptian sun god. It is my belief after years of study on this subject, that the root of most of the world's visible evil and wickedness is in the idolatry of sun worship (which is actually the worship of Lucifer). That is why I tie most of the spiritual difficulties we have in the United States of America to freemasonry — it is simply sun worship and thus the worship of satan himself, and it is rooted in America's formation. However, it goes deeper than America's formation as we know her today, as the First Nations people on this continent were, to a great extent, sun worshipers. In other words, the earth under our feet on this North American continent has soaked up the curses of sun worship for thousands of years. Again, *rasha* (the Hebrew for *wickedness*) and *ra* (the Hebrew for *evil* and the name of the Egyptian sun god) I believe are related words and concepts.

There are times when it is God's intent to use the whirlwind — storms — to deal with foundational wickedness. Proverbs 1:23-31, specifically verse 27, gives us a pretty clear picture of how we could actually oppose God in praying against the storm.

This passage is well worth the read for someone interested in praying about the weather. May we allow Holy Spirit direct us, as Romans 8:26 & 27 teach us to do, so that we know how to pray in accordance with what is in the heart of God as we continue to pray against the storm.

Chapter 14

Another Storm Story: Hurricane Ivan

I do not know why Ivan the Terrible was called by that name. I do not really know anything about Ivan the Terrible. As I'm getting ready to reconstruct this journal I think of the person called Ivan the Terrible. Though I do not know any of the details of that 16th century Tsar of Russia, I do know that Hurricane Ivan was terrible — a terror — to many, in Grenada, the Grenadines, and other islands of the Caribbean.

In May 2004 Denie and I took our first trip to the Caribbean. It was our 10th anniversary celebration and we went to Barbados and stayed on the south side of the island. As we always do, we made it a working vacation. As I remember, God was formulating the prenatal program and planting the beginnings of our prenatal prayer journal in our minds on this particular trip.

As we were enjoying our last evening on that beautiful island and getting ready to leave Barbados and return home the next morning, I went out and stood on the beach with my guitar and worshipped for about an hour and a half. In the dark of the night, hearing the waves against the shore, I felt like I was warring against some kind of monster or demonic structure in the Caribbean.

I continued to just worship and ask God to let the sound of worship invade the waters and follow the confluence of the currents and the waves through the Caribbean, into the Atlantic, and all the way to Africa. Again, I was feeling very much like I was warning against some sort of huge supernatural sea monster — a very real, and very realistic — feeling.

While we were in Barbados, my friend Ricardo Taylor and I had a conversation about hurricanes. His words were, "…hurricanes never hit Barbados. We haven't had a hurricane in over 50 years come near us. We're too far south in the Atlantic for their track that they make when they form off the coast of west Africa." I felt some comfort in that because we were entering hurricane season the week we were down there for that trip.

Now forward to September of that same year — I was shocked to hear the weather reports that a hurricane was headed for Barbados — a hurricane from West Africa named Ivan. My reaction was "…No! Ricardo said hurricanes don't hit Barbados." I immediately began to pray that God would shift this hurricane and either send it south of Barbados or north but spare that beautiful island that we just visited, and our friends. He did — the hurricane went south and edged Barbados but did no damage. However, it literally devastated Grenada and the Grenadine Islands, including the island of Carriacou, the home of other friends that we would meet — Pastor Happy and Denise Akasie.

We met them through a lady named Jenny, a resident of Barbados who formed a non profit ministry to help the devastated Grenadine Islands after Hurricane Ivan.
As this hurricane did it's damaged but spared the island of Barbados, I felt again — and was reminded again — of the "sea monster" I had warred against in Barbados on the beach that night back in May.

This same weekend as Ivan was ravaging the Caribbean, my wife and I had planned a meeting in Destin, Florida with a couple who were looking at our prenatal program and Early Childhood Music® program, to start teaching in their home area. This prenatal program was the same one God was giving birth to in our spirits while we were vacationing in Barbados four months earlier. Interestingly, this couple was from Barbados and had moved to Destin and were part of the Christian International ministry there at Santa Rosa Beach Florida. Denie and I were both so disappointed — and I was angry — because they had to cancel our meeting to stay home and board up their house so it was protected from a hurricane — Hurricane Ivan. Yes, this is the same hurricane that had nearly just hit Barbados. Now I was *really* beginning to feel that this was a personal attack on Denie and me, and our ministry, as a result of my worship and warfare against that demonic structure in the Caribbean, that night on the south shore of Barbados.

As we saw our weekend changed and that meeting canceled — by the way, it's never been rescheduled — Denie and I began to hear weather reports that the track of the hurricane was going to leave the coast and head up the state of Alabama. We realized that it it could blow right over our house. In the days following hurricane Ivan blowing over Destin, Florida that is exactly what happened. I remember praying for God to support and keep from breaking and falling on our house, the 50 foot hackberry trees that surrounded our home on the Tennessee River. And He did just that while, what had become by then tropical storm force winds, blew over them and caused them to bend and whirl in the storm. I had never in my life remembered experiencing any hurricane or tropical storm, much less those type of sustained winds in North Alabama, but here we were on this day experiencing them.

By now I was more than convinced that Hurricane Ivan was a direct result of my warfare and intercession since it targeted our friends in Barbados, our friends in Destin and our meeting, and then our very home. I said to Denie, "If this hurricane turns east and goes over North Carolina where our daughter is then I know it was formed and directed at us." To my jaw-dropping astonishment that's exactly what happened next.

Then I said, as the remains of Hurricane Ivan went out to sea at the Atlantic coast, "If this hurricane turns south and goes back around the coast of Florida and out to San Antonio, Texas where are son is stationed in the Air Force, then I **know** that it is a direct target on us.

That is exactly what Hurricane Ivan did — it turned south off the East Atlantic coast, then East and across the state of Florida where my wife's sister lived, then picked up intensity again as it went through the Gulf of Mexico and made landfall again in Texas, headed toward or directly over where our son was.

To say that I was astonished by all this is such an understatement. I couldn't believe what I had witnessed with Hurricane Ivan. I began to do research about hurricanes and this is what I found:

> The word hurricane is an English derivative of the name given to violent and devastating storms that the Arawak Indians of the Caribbean used to experience. They called any storm like this "*jurican*" (pronounced yur-i-cane), and they feared them as gods or demons. I realized immediately that we had been dealing with the demon that formed these type of swirling, circulating storms.

I also realized that Caribbean hurricanes are given birth to off the coast of west Africa. It is my strong opinion that hurricanes are formed through the witchcraft, voodoo and black magic of Africa and sent toward the Caribbean and the United States to do their devastation. We have to bear in mind that the circulating winds of hurricanes are, as tornadoes, whirlwinds. Remember that God uses whirlwinds to deal with His enemies — He sends the whirlwind against wickedness, against those who scoff at His Word and reject His knowledge.

This is found in Bible passages such as Psalm 58:3-9, Proverbs 1:23-33 & 10:25, Isaiah 40:24; 41:16 & 66:15-16, Jeremiah 23:19 & 30:23 and Nahum 1:3.

This being the case, any prayer and intercession strategy that works against tornadoes will also work against hurricanes. We can bind the spirit behind the storm or riding the storm — we can redirect the storms — we can ask the Father to touch the core of the storms and we can then break them up, just as we can any other storm. If we desire what the Father desires, and if He gives faith for it, we can live in authority over hurricanes just as we can other types of storms. I have seen this done recently — most recently with hurricane Irma. I felt directed to pray that God would break that storm up and send it in five directions that needed rain. As that storm hit the coast of Alabama and the Mobile and New Orleans area it began to widen, break up, and weaken, and it sent rain to multiple locations.

I was in a great learning process with Hurricane Ivan in 2004. Since then I have had many occasions to pray regarding hurricanes. Let God use you when you, or those you pray for, are in a fearful or threatening situation, to be a source of peace just as Jesus was during the storm.
As the old hymn says:

> *"The winds and the waves shall obey My will, peace be still.*
> *Whether the wrath of the storm-tossed sea*
> *Or demons or men or whatever it be,*
> *No water can swallow the ship where lies…*

The Master of ocean and earth and skies.
They all sweetly obey My will.
Peace be still, peace be still.
They all shall sweetly obey My will, peace, peace be still."

If He's at the helm of your ship, or asleep in the lower deck, you carry His authority over any storm **to direct it according to His will and purpose**. So take heart and be encouraged as you continue to pray against the storm.

Images of Hurricane Ivan 2004

Below are images of the track of Hurricane Ivan, images that stunned my wife and I as we watched this storm rage and war against our lives, those of our family and friends, and our mission:

From Weather Underground

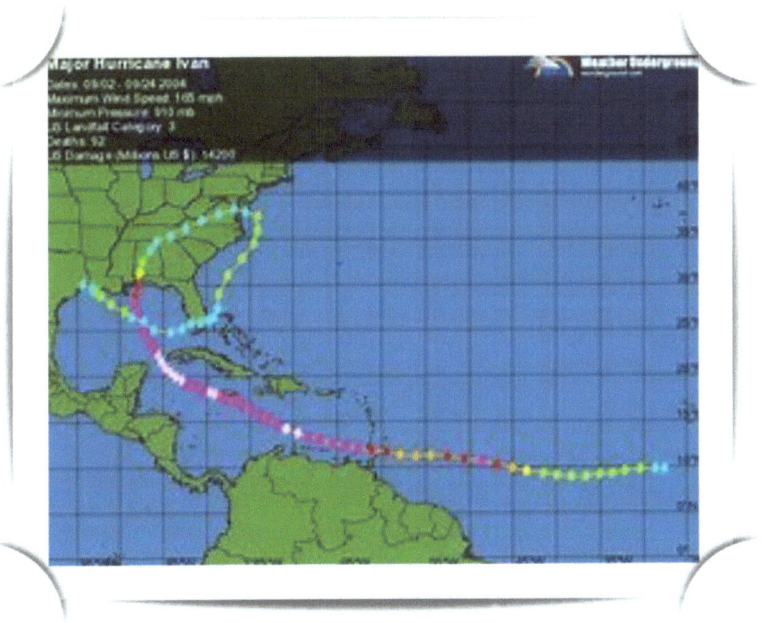

From nasa.gov

From Wikipedia.com

Chapter 15

Science Falsely So-called

An intriguing phrase to me, from the KJV Bible, has always been what Paul wrote in 1 Timothy 6:20 — to avoid vain and profane babbling and "science falsely so called."

I love that admonition!!!

What does this have to do with a book about weather? This has much to do with a book about weather, or prayer regarding weather. I'll talk about the reason why momentarily, but first…

To understand what Paul was saying we need to understand it in the original Greek text. The word science is the Greek word "gnosis", which means "to know, knowledge, intelligence". It is specifically used to speak of "knowledge of the Christian religion". It is a word used to refer to the knowledge of truth.

The words "falsely so called" come from the Greek word *pseudōnymos* — in other words, to be falsely named — a pseudonym. Paul was saying, under inspiration of Holy Spirit, that some of what is called science is given a false name.

Paul was saying to Timothy that there is *fake science*. Science that is based on a lie is not science at all… it defies the very meaning and definition of science.

Any science that is based upon a system that has bought into a lie CANNOT be accurate science. In other words, it is *science falsely so called*. It's whole premiss is based upon a lie and is rooted in and built upon blindness to the truth.

Much of science today is based upon a rejection of the Word of God as the truth. It is based upon a rejection of the very words of Jesus in John 17:17 in which He said to God the Father, "… Your Word is truth". In other words, "God, Your written Word (*logos*) to man is truth." Science has for years — decades — centuries — millennia rejected the Word of God as His truth to man. Science that is based upon a system, thought process, organization, person or group of people that have rejected God's Word as truth is founded in a lie and deception and <u>can be nothing but a deception because the proponents of it are deceived</u>. So, it is gross misjudgment to base any life-changing or life directing belief on science based upon a lie — false science.

False Science and Weather

There is a fallacy in much of weather related science. This science is based upon a system of idolatry — false worship. It is forged by those who are either committed to, or deceived by, spirits of idolatry and error.

These people are guilty of the age old idolatry of worshipping creation instead of the Creator (Romans 1:25). This has been satan's scheme since he tempted Eve in the Garden of Eden. He himself is part of God's creation, and he wants to be the object of our worship.

He will try to get us to worship the creation God made rather than God Himself — the Creator. In doing so he is diverting worship from God. Those who worship "mother earth" are worshipping the creature/creation rather than the Creator — and I believe they are in effect worshiping satan himself, because he is the author of this idolatry, and is part of the creation being worshiped.

Stewards of Creation

This is not to say that there is not a need to take care of the earth as God's creation. He made it for us and we are His appointed stewards of it (Psalm 115:16). It is a terrible tragedy to neglect to take care of God's creation that He gave us to maintain. I cringe when I see Civil War era photos of the southern United States and how the land was raped of forests and trees and left bare, just as I cringed when I went to Haiti and saw the same thing on the land there. But it is just as much a tragedy to be deceived into a false doctrine that says we cannot avail ourselves of the vast riches God put in the earth to benefit mankind because man is somehow destroying the climate by harvesting these resources. It is my belief that the science that says that man is altering the climate by the use of natural resources is "science falsely so called".

I believe it is an attempt by any <u>sincere</u> believer in this, to correct a real problem of neglect of our planet by a wrong means or strategy. I also believe that there are those promoting this false science who are doing so for other reasons and with other motivations, and in the process robbing the riches God put in the earth (Psalm 104:24) from those who should rightly receive and make use of them, while themselves profiting greatly and benefiting from what they would deprive others of.

I do believe there is climate change, or shifts in the climate. This would be more regional than global. It could also be the result of shifts in the spiritual climate in a region or nation, and could be a positive change or a negative change. My eyes were opened to this when I was having a conversation with our mayor about the frequency of rain in our region. I found myself saying to him that "...we need to take advantage of all the rain we're having and ask God how we should steward all the water, and bless other areas with it, because this is going to continue since we are experiencing a climate change." I did not plan to use the word climate change — it took me by surprise that I had used it. Because I've never bought into that thinking I had my attention captured by the fact that I did use that phrase. This whole conversation and experience was, I believe, the result of an experience I had in which intercession was the tool used to break severe draught in Alabama. During that period of time (2011-2013) the Lord spoke to me and told me that He was making Huntsville, Alabama (my city) into an Eden.

This all was part of His revealing to me that it was His desire to bring an end to sun worship and that I was to decree "the beginning of the end" of sun worship. During that time, through seeking God in prayer and Bible study, and doing numerous prayer assignments related to this study, I came to believe that it was God's intent for the earth to be much like a productive rain forest — as the Garden of Eden would have been — and that sun worship had brought a curse upon the earth and any region given to such false worship. We have begun to see this broken off the region where I live. I believe this trend will continue, though the warfare in the spirit realm continues also.

Again, this is an evidence of positive climate change. There can also be negative climate change, much like the midwest plains of the United States experienced in the 1930's in what is referred to as the "Dust Bowl".

I use this above illustrations in this particular book to demonstrate how climate change can occur, and how it can be altered if need be.

Praying in Truth-Praying in the Spirit

How does false science affect praying against the storm? The simple and short answer is, we've got to know the source were dealing with in the spirit realm before we can stop anything that's going on of adversity in the natural realm. We have to know if there is a lying spirit at work, and spirits of idolatry, and witchcraft, related to the false science of weather.

If we do not know, or accept this — if we do not know what entity were up against — we cannot win the battle. This precedent is given in Scripture and Jesus Himself used this precedent. This is rooted in God's concept that light manifests and then expels or dismantles darkness. It is rooted in the same concept that forgiveness and cleansing requires confession — acknowledging and admitting — first.

The essence of science is knowledge — i.e. to know. Most of the references I hear about science in the modern world have to do with gaining knowledge, or a "learning by experimentation" concept — a progressive knowledge. That is NOT Biblical knowledge, rather it is fulfillment of what Paul wrote in 2 Timothy 3:7 of those who were "… ever learning but never able to come to the knowledge of the truth". The knowledge God talks about in the Bible is one of starting with the assumption that He is right and we need to learn why what *He* says is true and accurate, and why His ways are the right ways. The Hebrew mindset is to accept that God is right whether I understand or not, and then try to come to an understanding. The Greek mindset is to come to an understanding before I believe or accept a thing as truth, and today's "science" is based upon this Greek mindset — braggingly so. This is idolatry, and it is strong idolatry. It actually is rooted in the system of the Greek gods. There is a concept presented in Zachariah 9:13 that those who seek to know truth would do well to understand… it is that the *"sons of Zion will oppose the sons of Greece"*. In other words, the Hebrew mindset is in opposition to the Greek mindset.

The root of this is in the unseen world — it is in a spiritual world and Zachariah's reference is to a spiritual war with two opposing sides. It is interesting that the Greek mindset is to not accept anything one cannot see, hear, touch, smell, feel — connect with using the physical senses. The Hebrew mindset is to accept what God (a Spirit) says and orders, and then seek for His understanding — which He is very willing to give at need and in the appropriate time, to those who submit to His wisdom. It is also interesting that it was to those of the Hebrew mindset that God gave the inspired Word of God (Romans 3:2; Hebrews 5:12).

Most of science today, especially related to weather, is of the Greek mindset and further is of the 2 Timothy 3:7 variety, vacillating back and forth from one extreme to the next but not ever able to confirm what is said to be science. I heard one man use a phrase I like, and think fits well here to describe such: They are about *"… as confused as a termite in a yoyo…"*

As people of prayer, we cannot hope to see our prayers answered as related to disarming storms and adverse weather conditions if we do not pray in accordance with God's will. Praying in the will of God is described in Romans as praying according to the mind of the Spirit of God. Romans 8:26 & 27 describe a scenario in which God and Holy Spirit confer on what is in God's mind so that Holy Spirit can convey that to us, so we can pray accordingly. Holy Spirit actually wants to help us frame our prayer in such a way that God is sure to answer it because we are praying the mind of God.

This is praying in the Spirit! We, as God's authority in our part of the earth then, bring God's desire into the earth by our prayers and decrees.

Some of the Fears

Many people live in a state of panic. The enemy of God — satan — who is also our enemy, wants to keep us in that state… he wants to keep us in fear. He sends out spirits of fear to give birth to all kinds of fears. There are many fears floated these days as to whether or not man is responsible for global climate change. Can man's actions cause the climate to change permanently? I don't claim to know the answer to that. I also know that neither does anyone else alive know the answer to that (at least on a long term basis), because weather patterns have not been monitored enough centuries to know that answer. One thing I am sure of is that man's actions have, down through history, caused God to alter the climate, or at least allow it to be altered. This was true after man was cast out of the Garden of Eden. This was true during the great flood in Noah's time. This was true after the flood, in that man lived under a canopy of moisture before the flood. I believe that was much like a tropical rain forest. After the flood the canopy was removed allowing the sun to be seen in all it's brightness. I know that God is in ultimate control of all climate and weather and He can either send, assign, or alter climate and weather based upon man's heart and actions. I also know that God has given to man the authority to reverse or alter weather that is adverse.

One of the above mentioned fears is that the world is coming to an end. This fear has been around all my life — for 6 decades I've heard one theory after another as to why the world is nearing an end.

This I know: God created the earth and it will abide forever (Ecclesiastes 1:4; Psalm 119:90). The earth is perpetual. God made it to be so. Though the earth has been polluted terribly by man — which is disgraceful — God has His way of restoring earth (Isaiah 65:17; 66:22; Matthew 17:11; Acts 3:21; 2 Peter 3:10-13; Revelation 21:1).

Another fear has to do with the rising of the seas. This was prophesied in Scripture, in Ezekiel 26:15-21 we see the Lord God, Jehovah, foretelling of a great sea power civilization being covered by the waves of the sea, both the coastlines and the islands. My question to those who fear the rising of the seas encroaching on our coastlines is, did you not think Jesus knew what He was talking about in Matthew 7:24-29 when He used the analogy of the wise man who built his house on a rock, as opposed to the foolish man who built on the sand. And what a great analogy of this entire "false science" discussion — those who listen to the Word of God and obey are like those who build upon a rock. Those who hear the Word of God and do not obey, Jesus likens to a man who builds his house on the sand. What folly to build at sea level and near the shore, then panic when unpredictable seas rise — seas whose tides have always been unpredictable since God created them.

Something that is of great comfort to me and should be to anyone living near water is the fact that Psalm 104:9 teaches us that God restrains the waters according to His covenant. This principle is stated again in Proverbs 8:29. Psalm 104:9 says that God has set a boundary that waters may not pass over, and thus may not cover the earth again.

This is a reference to the rainbow that God set in the sky after the flood as a sign of His promise to not cover the earth again with water. The Hebrew word used for "bound" or boundary is the word *gebul* and it means a chord. By extension it means the boundary or territory within the chord. It then means "border, boundary, coast, landmark, limit, quarter or space". Proverbs 8:29 says that God has given a command to the waters and decreed their boundaries and they cannot cross over His commanded boundary. God has assigned to the seas — the waters — their space and they are limited to the area within that boundary. It is only in the Lord's will then, that waters are allowed to rise to any level. Man gets really close to idolatry when He assumes that He can control the rise or fall of waters. Though we have developed dams, canal systems, retainer ponds, etc… over the centuries, we would do well to remember that this is all in God's control and we need to build our lives a safe enough distance from water if we want ensured safety.

The Seasons of the Lord

A huge underlying component of the "climate change" or "global warming" discussion and fear has to do with the changing of seasons. In some places, in some years, the seasons are more and more merging into each other and we are seeing less obvious seasonal change. This seems to be on an alternating basis year by year where I live. This has been the trend I've observed all my life in the deep south of the United States, though I am more aware of it now because of the current political discussion of global warming.

There are basically two seasons in Scripture — they are "seed time and harvest". Coming out of the flood God made covenant with Noah (Genesis 8:20-9:18). In that covenant God confirmed that there would always be, as long as the earth stands, the two seasons of the year — seedtime and harvest. These are tied to heat and cold and are also called summer and winter (Genesis 8:22). Actually it could be said that the rainbow is God's sign of covenant that the earth will always have seedtime and harvest coupled with a warm, growing season and a cold, dormant season. To try to define weather, climate or whatever one chooses to call it, more rigidly than this on a longterm basis is to try to play God and predict or orchestrate something He — the Creator — never designed, ordained or promised. Maybe in that last statement I've just hit on the root of the problem. Here is the Word of God on this matter…

"While the earth remains seedtime and harvest, cold and heat, winter and summer, and day and night shall not cease" and "… the earth abides forever."(Genesis 8:22-NKJV; Ecclesiastes 1:4) However, since these promises are tied to covenant, when mankind decides to ignore God's covenant that He's made with us it may very well be in His mind to allow or send the altering of the effects of that covenant so as to get man's attention. This could be one explanation of unusual climate trends… I believe it is.

I know that in the region in which I live we have seen a changing climate for the past 8 years.

It's as if there is a struggle going on for the land in the southern United States to become more of a rainy place and less one of extreme sunshine. I have been engaged in this heavily since 2011, as I have explained earlier in this chapter. God desires to — God is — dismantling and doing away with sun worship. I am convinced this is at the core of the changing climate in North Alabama and Southern Tennessee where I live.

Oppositions of Science

As mentioned earlier, Paul wrote in 1 Timothy 6:20 telling us to, "…avoid… oppositions of science falsely so-called." The Greek word for *oppositions* is *antithesis*. i.e. false science is the antithesis of science. The definition of antithesis is *the direct opposite* of a thing. Pseudo-science, or science based upon a false narrative is the direct opposite of science.

This is easy to understand since the very definition of science is knowledge, or to know. The negative effect is the opposition… opposition to truth. False science is just a another way for the enemy of God, the prince of darkness who is the god of this world — satan — to deceive and keep people from knowing the truth of God and His Word. False science opposes God and His truth. False science is a huge part of what satan tries to use to blind the minds of people that are educated in science and put their faith in science, to damn their souls for eternity.

False science has no place in the life or mind of one of God's intercessors who would be His tool in praying against the storm or interrupting or redirecting foul weather.

It misdirects our intercession and takes us out of praying in the will of God — praying what Jesus is praying — and sends us down a path to no avail. Prayer based upon falsehood, not founded in truth, is a worthless futile effort. The exception to this is the fact that, to those seeking God's truth, Holy Spirit will direct their minds in the direction of truth and away from error, so that they eventually arrive at the truth.

The 1 Corinthians 1 and 2 Effect

Proverbs 28:5 states that "Evil men do not understand judgement (justice, righteous judgement, God's decisions); but they that seek the Lord understand all things." God hides His wisdom from those who don't have a desire for His heart.

He hides His wisdom from those who scoff at His wisdom. Frankly, I don't blame Him. He makes His wisdom — the wisdom of the Creator — available to us freely, but at great cost to Him. It cost Him His Son's life. It also cost those prophets who were inspired to write the Word of God their lives in many situations. I can understand why God would hide His wisdom from those who scoff at it and reject it. God's wisdom is such a valuable commodity.

That God hides His wisdom from those who scoff at it and/or reject it, is a truth presented in multiple places in Scripture. I want to discuss three of those references here:

> In 1 Corinthians chapters 1 and 2 Paul goes to great lengths to explain that those who reject as their premise the wisdom of God are left to stumble in their own foolishness. In John's Biblical writing he described it as stumbling in darkness. When someone rejects the wisdom of God and does not accept that God is right and that we need to conform to what He has said in His Word, then God orchestrates that person's life so that they walk in deception — the very deception they have chosen (2 Corinthians 4:4; 2 Thessalonians 2:8-12; 1 Peter 2:6-8; 2 Peter 3:16). God actually says in 1 Peter 2:8 that those who reject Jesus — God's chief cornerstone or, the foundation of all God set in motion at creation — have an appointment with deception, darkness, stumbling, disobedience, and

the destruction which accompanies this. Jesus is the representation of the Word of God to man in the earth, so for one to reject Jesus is synonymous with rejecting the Word of God, and vice-versa.

There is a very interesting story in the Old Testament that validates the argument I'm making here. In 1 Kings 22:19-23 we see the story of God calling for spirits, gathered at His council, to go and deceive Ahab, who was the epitome of the rejection of God's Word. God used His created spirit beings to set up Ahab to be deceived by those lying spirits so that he would walk right into a death trap. This is not because God is evil or wants the demise of people He has created.

It is, rather, because He has established a principle — a judgement — that when someone rejects His Word they reject life and thus have an appointment with death. God has magnified His Word above all His name (Psalm 138:2) and there is no part of God's nature that He will put above the keeping of His Word — God will not compromise His Word, so He has staked His name on it. Ahab died because he chose to reject the wisdom of the Word of God. When he made that choice he automatically chose to be deceived and led into his demise.

The same idea is presented in Proverbs 1:23-33. The wisdom and knowledge of God lead us into and through life. In this passage we see God pouring out Holy Spirit and His Word to us to give us a chance to run to it and find life, health and safety. Those who reject God's outpouring are found in calamity, destruction and death.

The author James got a picture of this from God and wrote about it under inspiration from Holy Spirit. In James 3:13-18 we get a revelation of the fact that some wisdom comes from above and some from below. The wisdom from above is of God and is for the establishing of the Kingdom of God and its righteousness and peace which is designed to bless all people of the earth. The wisdom from below is earthly, fleshly and demonic, to put it plainly — to put it just as James put it. As with Ahab, that devilish wisdom leads to deception, lies and then death.

One of the oft repeated concepts in the book of Proverbs is that those who scoff at the Word of God, who mock at it, are destined to walk through life without wisdom. They seek wisdom but it eludes them... they never find the wisdom and answers they look for because they scoff at God's Word. He has laid out His wisdom in the Bible and those who mock the Bible are mocking the very wisdom of God, so God let's them stumble on in darkness and the stupidity of their unbelief.

Now back to the discussion at hand. I have gone to great pains to write this chapter because is is imperative, if we're going to get our prayers answered, that we pray according to truth and according to the heart of God. If we are praying based upon a false narrative then we are praying based upon a lie. If we pray based upon fear then we are praying based upon something birthed in our minds by a spirit that is not of God (2 Timothy 1:7). My life is given to helping people find shalom and living in shalom means overcoming adverse weather at times. I felt it important to include this chapter in such a book. May God lead you as to how to pray according to truth and according to His heart, against the storms you encounter.

Chapter 16

The Personification of Storms

I believe — I have experienced — that storms have personality. I've had storms rush at me — or at least winds released by certain storms — on more than one occasion. I have experienced storms form and track over several days that targeted areas of my life, and people in my life. I have felt presences in storms or before the formation of storms that I believe were engaging me. Storms have, from my experience, personalities.

Those storms that I have engaged with in prayer certainly have displayed this. I believe many weather forecasters and observers would agree that storms have personalities, though I've never discussed it with any of them. I think it is interesting that storms are given names — the names of persons. I think that acknowledging that the personification of storms is a fact is important for those who, through prayer, intend on engaging, changing or stopping those storms. I do state this is a fact — not a scientifically proven fact, but a fact demonstrated by the reality that exists with storms and those who engage them in the spirit realm.

From a Biblical standpoint, storms take on the personality of the spirit that is riding them, and use their force for their own purpose.

This is true of storms ridden by sprits of darkness to do harm, damage and devastation, and bring fear — it is also true of those storms whose winds and clouds God (a Spirit) chooses to ride (2 Samuel 22:11; Psalm 18:10; 104:3). I believe God also dispatches His angels to ride storms to carry out His purposes.

The definition of *personification* is to "attribute personal nature or human characteristics to something nonhuman, or to represent an abstract quality in human form". Some terms used as synonymous with *personification* are: embodiment, epitome, incarnation, essence, archetype, paradigm, type, symbol, prototype, representation, soul, picture, model, symbolization, exemplification, image, example, avatar.

Now what comes to my mind as I write the above synonyms is that God chose Jesus to be the "express image of His person" (Hebrews 1:3). The original Greek word used for *express image* is *charakter* and it means "to be stamped with someone's image, or the exact copy of, as by engraving…"

This thought process, applied to the thinking that storms can take on personality, is a powerful visual. Storms can act as entities with personalities. They can either seek to achieve good or bad depending upon the personality they have taken on. In the case presented in this book, ALL STORMS should be conformed to an image that carries out the will and Word of God. You and I are ones who hold the authority to make that happen.

Here are some examples of storms that I have seen *personified*... that is, take on a personality.

> Hurricane Ivan: As I have written in a previous chapter, Hurricane Ivan in 2004 took on a personality all it's own in opposing things God has called my wife and I to, and people in our lives that we love. I am convinced it started as a result of intercession and worship I engaged in.
>
> On April 27, 2011 a tornado sent out a *finger* lunging at me. This happened as I was directing *with my finger*, and commanding the tornado to move away from our house and out of our neighborhood.
>
> On Halloween, October 31, 2013, I was engaging in a weekly practice of binding witchcraft on a high place near our home. A wind cam raging down the mountain (Panther Knob, south of Monte Sano Mountain in Huntsville, Alabama) and toward me, picked up a heavy metal swing and threw it at me.

These are three very prominent examples in my life, and the basis for the reason I include this short chapter in this book. I do so not to be dramatic — I do so to emphasize the point that weather systems can be inhabited (ridden) by spiritual forces that wish to stop us from accomplishing the tasks God has assigned us. As people of God who wish to do His Kingdom's work it is important that we recognize what is happening and exercise the authority of Jesus over the spiritual forces using weather to try to stop us.

I encourage you to live with the mindset that "I am in authority here (*here* being wherever you are in the will of God), and you (storm) are not going to do that here!" I remind you of passages like Genesis 1:26 & 28, Psalm 8:6; 107:29; 115:16, Daniel 7:27 an Mark 4:39. Let the authority of Jesus over nature be alive in you as you **pray against the storm.**

Chapter 17

Another Storm Story: Richard Parker's Testimony

As I was completing the writing of this book, I was having a phone conversation with a couple of friends I used to work with in radio. I was talking to them about this book and one of them, Richard Parker, said, "... I need to send you a picture of a weather map that I copied, of the day my wife was praying for our daughter who was driving in severe weather." I asked Richard if he would write a testimony of that experience and send it with the weather map picture. Richard's testimony is below and with it the picture of the path God cut in the storms that day to protect his daughter as she drove.

> *"Weather anxiety started for my wife, Amy, not long after we moved to north Alabama from South Georgia in 1978. One year later we left early one morning for a trip to visit family in Georgia and found ourselves right in the middle of a tornado just 30 minutes into our journey. That was before the days of much advance warning of severe weather. The experience was so traumatic that our family became weather prayer warriors from that day on.*

Fast forward to March 2, 2012. I had a wedding to perform in Sylacauga, Alabama that weekend and my daughter Leah, was driving from Tuscaloosa, Alabama to join me for the event. Weather forecasters were calling that day a weather alert day because of the possibility of severe storms across the state. Amy immediately started praying for safety for Leah's trip. That afternoon the weather started to get bad across the state and our prayer was for a safe passage for our daughter from Tuscaloosa to Sylacauga.

I was watching the statewide weather radar as Leah was traveling and I was amazed at what I saw. As you can see in the picture (below) from that day, there were rotating storms north and south but the path of our daughter's trip was completely clear for over 60 miles on either side of her during her entire journey. Yes, God is in charge of the storms and he does answer our prayers to give us safe journey in our travels."

~Richard Parker

From intellicast.com from Weather Undrground

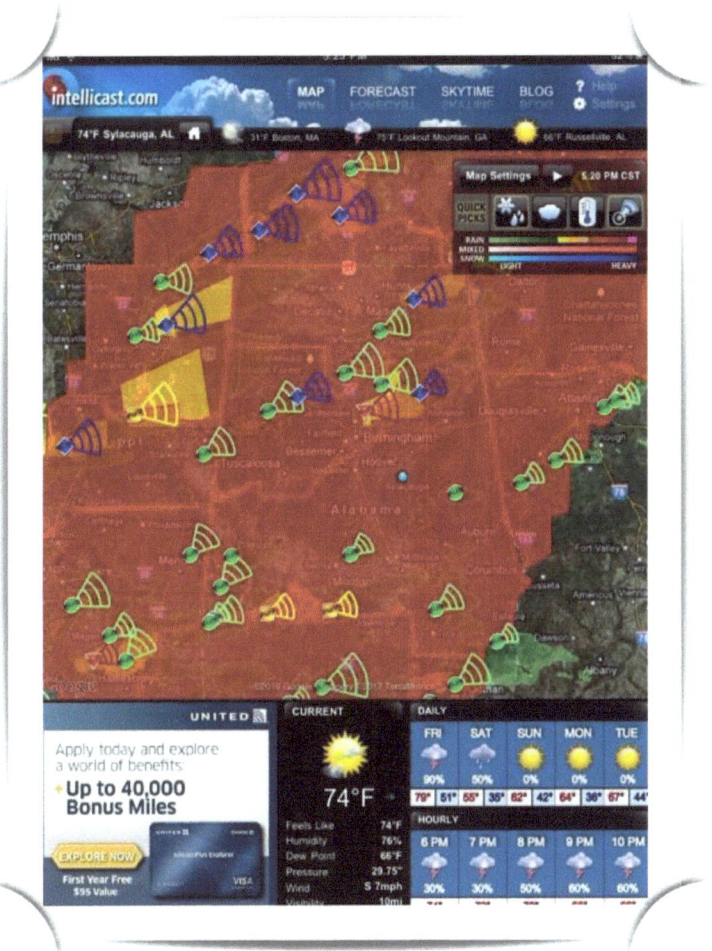

My thanks to Richard Parker for sharing that testimony. I've chosen to end this book with his storm story. I wanted to subtitle his testimony as "The Path of the Righteous", but I felt that would be taking liberties with what Richard actually wrote, so I chose not to do so.

The day mentioned in the story above reminds me of Proverbs 4:18. This verse is in a context that is talking about the violence that the wicked must suffer, and even walk in as a manner of life. It is as if they ingest violence, as they *drink the wine of violence*. Then verse 18 says, *"…but the path of the just (righteous) is as a shining light that shines brighter and brighter unto the perfect day."* God wants to light our path and direct us into His place of safety and protection — a place of shalom. He does so for those who look to Him for that. He will answer your prayer for protection, even in the most severe of circumstances. He will cut a path of safety and light for you to walk in, just as is evidenced in Richard's picture of the weather map. He will give you the same peace — the same shalom — Jesus knew, in any storm.

God bless you and inspire you as you continue to **pray against the storm**.

Conclusion

God does not want us to live in fear but in confidence (Jeremiah 29:11). Go wants us to live in peace — shalom. Jesus wants us to live in peace. He is our example of peace and His life was that of complete shalom, as He was able to navigate Himself through any circumstance standing in the confidence of God.

This book is written to give instruction and examples of how storms have and continue to be altered, disarmed, moved or encountered with no or minimal harm. It is written to give comfort to those who live in a fear or dread of storms, as I did the first 4 decades of my life. The writing of this book comes as a result of a six year prayer assignment I was given when I was a radio announcer and had to give weather reports and updates regularly. It's writing was assigned to me in part because of the assignment on my life of being what Proverbs 12:20 calls "…a counselor of shalom".

This book is about storms, which can be devastating things. However, they exist to carry out the Word or will or mandate of God Himself. Psalm 148 says that "stormy winds fulfill His Word…" So it is God's intent that storms obey His will — His heart's desire — His plan and design, and that they bring other things and people into alignment with that same design.

The Hebrew word used for the above word *fulfill* is *asah* — it is the word used to describe action as in doing, carrying out, maintaining, fulfilling, etc… it describes work. Any winds, or storms, are intended by God to carry out His desire expressed in His Word — either the written Word of God or a word that He gives in the immediate to ultimately fulfill His written Word. Any storms that fight against the will of God and the Word of God are fighting against God himself. When we encounter those types of storms, we have the authority in Jesus name to put a stop to their opposition to what God desires. As we have talked about in this book, we can either reroute them, dismantle them, break them up into small pieces, lift them out of reach — in short, put a stop to them. Any storms that fight against our carrying out, fulfilling or obeying the Word of God or God's assignments to us, we have the authority in Jesus' name to stop.

A good example of this would be an incident that my wife and I encountered in July 2002. We had been stirred in a conference early that year to pray about racial healing, something we had long been passionate about. While taking a vacation trip to Cherokee, North Carolina we were meditating on what was shared at the conference and listening to those messages on tape again. During all of this we were led to believe that before there could be racial healing for slavery and issues of black and white racism there had to also be reconciliation made for the wrongs done to Native American Indians — the first inhabitants and stewards of our land.

We prayed and sought God's heart for our role in that and determined that we were to make our W.C. Handy Festival emphasis that year one of recognition of the fact that Native Americans were the first people to inhabit and steward the land we call home, and that we owed them much for what we had inherited, and that our forefathers had wronged them greatly. We planned an event around this theme for July 2002. We wrote songs in dedication to this event. We had our students prepare performances around this theme. We prayer walked the park in which we were going to hold this event. We had an additional day of worship scheduled with praise bands from various churches. The day this event was to begin I was ministering on the radio while meditating on Psalm 68:32-35 — I was talking about God riding on the clouds and showing His strength in the heavens, and about the fact that the heavens are actually participants in *ascribing* strength to God, something we are here commanded to do. I made a statement to the effect that I that later that weekend I believed God was going to demonstrate His strength in the clouds at our event. Boy was I surprised the next day to see a squall line of storms heading toward our park pavilion, just as we were about to begin our event. As I took the stage to begin the worship event the Lord reminded me of what I'd said the day before on the radio. I took the microphone and began to pray and command the clouds to give way to the will of God and to demonstrate His strength and power, and not to interfere with what He had planned for our event. I then commanded the cloud system to weaken and brake up so that our event did not get interrupted.

That is exactly what happened — no hard rain and no strong or dangerous winds or lightening. Praise God! The morning after our event the front page of the local paper headlined with a picture of the park where we'd held the event, and the words "Peace in the Park".

A more recent example is as follows:

> Tuesday February 28, 2017, needing to shower before my weekly prayer drive, there was a pretty severe thunder storm over us with lots of lightening. I was under a fairly strict time constraint and did not want to wait until the storm passed over to get ready for the day. I simply said, "Father please stop all lightning within 8 miles of me till I finish my shower so I can go ahead and do what You want me to do." The lightening stopped instantly, and did not restart till I was out of the shower, dried off and finishing getting ready to leave. I heard a thunder clap signifying the restart of the storm as I was sitting to put my socks on. It was as if God was reminding me (He was) that He had answered my prayer. And He does…

We have authority over storms because God wants us to live in shalom (Psalm 85:8; Psalm 29:11; Jeremiah 29:11) AND, because He does not want our work for Him being hindered. The enemy will try to torment us with fear and steal our joy and peace because that thwarts our Kingdom work, as the Kingdom of God is joy and righteousness and peace in Holy Spirit.

And the enemy will outright try to stop our Kingdom work by interference through the storm. Again, he has watched God — his Creator — for millennia, ride the winds and clouds and he tries to mimic God and ride the clouds, in a perverse way and for perverse purposes. He tries that with everything God has done.

I remember well the awful feeling of dread on days when the skies looked threatening, or weather forecasters were giving out reports of threatening weather. I never want to — nor do I plan to — live under that dread again. I am called to live a life of shalom and to spread that mindset to others in my life and the region in which I live. This is an assignment to me by the Lord.

So I write this book to stir faith in your heart so that you know you have access to the same authority over storms that Jesus did, the One who created the elements that storms consist of.

Here are some important things to remember:

- One person with the faith of Jesus can bind any evil in any cloud system and loose it off themselves and those they are responsible for or pray for. If you're reading this and you question whether or not Jesus lives in you, to give you access to His authority, you may right now receive Him into your life as your Lord and Savior, and He will come to make His home in your being. (Romans 10:13; Romans 8:9-11; Ephesians 3:17; Revelation 3:20; 1 John 5:13). He longs to live in you and fill your life and all that it consists of with His amazing peace — His shalom. That includes His protection and His freedom from fear, for you and for those you love and pray for.

- One person with the faith of Jesus can command peace into a storm.

- A handful of people in a region can build a shield over that region so that there is shalom, even with the weather (Matthew 18:19).

- Enough people in a region, walking in the faith of Jesus, can put a shield over an entire region that cannot be penetrated by violent storms.

- Shalom is always the will of God. Violence, and the terror and fear that come from it, are from spirits that are not of God and Jesus died and rose to give His followers victory over those spirits. We have the power and authority over the demonic realm, and all the realm of spiritual darkness.

If there has ever been a time in history where Romans 8:22 is applicable that time is now. The whole creation and earth itself is crying out with "groans of calamity" for the children of God to take their place as mature sons and daughters of the Creator and enforce His will and purpose into the earth — into creation. Creation is waiting on you and me to step into the shoes of Jesus and enforce His way and His way ultimately leads us into His shalom. This is so clearly pictured for us in Psalm 85:4-13 and summarized in verse 13.

One of the most famous of Bible authors shared our fear of storms. David wrote about it in Psalm 55:8. "I would hasten my escape from the windy storm and tempest." We'd all love to never encounter a storm. That's not the way God made it. That's not what He ordained. His plan was for us to be in Christ's stead and exercise Jesus' authority over the storm. I hope this short book will be a tool of Holy Spirit to bring you closer to the heart of Jesus and grow your faith to the point that you will be a shield to those you love and serve, and to yourself, from the harm dangerous storms can bring. **God, may it be so?**

May you and I, as Jesus did, pray against the storm.

www.ingramcontent.com/pod-product-compliance
Lightning Source LLC
Chambersburg PA
CBHW041805160426
43191CB00004B/64